Homosexuality and the Bible

Outdated Advice or Words of Life?

R. Nicholas Black

New
Growth
Press

www.newgrowthpress.com

New Growth Press, Greensboro, NC 27404
www.newgrowthpress.com
Copyright © 2014 by Harvest USA

All Scripture quotations, unless otherwise indicated are from *The
Holy Bible, English Standard Version*® (ESV®), copyright © 2000,
2001 by Crossway Bibles, a division of Good News Publishers.
Used by permission. All rights reserved.

Cover Design: Faceout Books, faceoutstudio.com
Typesetting: Lisa Parnell, lparnell.com

ISBN: 978-1-939946-05-8 (Print)
ISBN: 978-1-939946-06-5 (eBook)

Library of Congress Cataloging-in-Publication Data
Black, R. Nicholas, 1955–
  Homosexuality and the Bible : outdated advice or words of life? /
R. Nicholas Black.
     pages cm
  ISBN 978-1-939946-05-8 (print) — ISBN 978-1-939946-06-5
(ebook) 1. Homosexuality—Religious aspects—Christianity. 2.
Homosexuality—Biblical teaching. 3. Bible—Criticism, interpre-
tation, etc. I. Title.
  BR115.H6B524 2014
  261.8'35766—dc23
                                                    2014026240

Printed in Canada

21 20 19 18 17 16 15 14   1 2 3 4 5

Jared said he was leaving the church, now that he was able to recognize and give voice to his same-sex attractions.

Tom thought he knew his friend Jared. They had known each other for several years as members of the same church. Both were actively involved in various church ministries. After their meeting, he realized he actually knew very little. Jared argued that God had made him gay, and he needed to be who he was. That meant he could not remain in their church because it was against accepting homosexuality and offered no place for someone like Jared, who wanted to be in a loving, committed relationship like heterosexuals in the church.

Tom attempted to counter Jared's position, but when the discussion centered on the Bible, things got even more confusing. Every Scripture passage Tom raised in an attempt to show Jared that engaging in a homosexual relationship was unbiblical, Jared countered with a different interpretation, insisting that the Scripture passages that touch upon homosexuality are no longer applicable to men and women who are same-sex attracted. It was a different time and a different place back then, he argued. Scripture focuses on love, and that was the central reason Jared was moving in this new direction. He was now free to seek love with a future partner, and be a Christian too.

❧

The world is changing. The speed with which change now occurs is faster than ever. And nothing is changing more rapidly than the way we understand sexuality and relationships. Homosexuality and its increasing acceptance, not just by society at large but also by people within the

3

Christian church, is challenging the way Christians have historically and doctrinally understood sex and its role in defining relationships. And this is not a mere intellectual debate; it is a battle that is beginning to tear apart even conservative and evangelical churches, denominations, families, and friendships. It is a battle with wide-ranging societal and faith implications.

It is a confusing time. Many Christian people and denominations are reinterpreting the church's long-held stance on Scripture passages—that is, the orthodox position. Some denominations are accepting gay and lesbian relationships as being fully sanctioned by God. And society at large is increasingly pressuring, if not silencing, any voice that does not affirm gay relationships.

Churches that hold to the orthodox position seem increasingly silent on the subject—not wanting the world to interpret their position on the subject as being the church's main message. While it's true that the gospel is about more than sexual ethics, the silence of the evangelical church (particularly at the local level) is contributing to the confusion about the role of Scripture to direct Christians in understanding and living out their lives and their sexuality in accordance with God's design.

People on both sides bring to the table passionate arguments and perspectives, with each side claiming they are being faithful to the biblical text. For those who desire to follow Jesus, it matters whether one obeys his will in this area. While spirituality today is considered to be whatever enriches or affirms one's life, for the Christian, the test of real faith has always been, and continues to be, obeying what God says. What is the truth of this important matter?

Creating a Safe Space for Discussion

It has been a long-held position throughout Christianity that the Scriptures are foundational texts that tell us who we are and how we are to live before God. People on both sides of this issue still believe this, but they differ widely in how they interpret the Bible. Let me suggest four ways to approach this discussion.

1. Don't use the Bible merely to win an argument. This is not a debate about some abstract, theological principle; this is about people. Sexuality touches on the core of who we are and how we relate to others, and conversations surrounding it should be handled with great care. There is a lot of confusion today over what the Bible says about homosexuality and many reasons for that confusion. We need to keep in mind that there are men and women in our churches who live with same-sex attractions—and many of them struggle with this secretly. Many of them are confused when they read these passages about whether or not God truly loves them—and especially when they hear heterosexual Christians discussing the passages. These men and women want to know how to live before God in accordance to his revealed will. Sensitivity, care, and compassion ought to shape the tone of this discussion with everyone.

2. While it's not about winning an argument, it's also not about drawing a line between "them" and "us." When we discuss whether or not homosexuality is acceptable before God, those

who are heterosexual must include themselves in this discussion. When the Scripture discusses homosexuality, it does so in the context of sexuality overall. It doesn't say homosexuality is broken and heterosexuality isn't. Everyone experiences broken sexuality at some level.

In fact, there are far more verses in the Bible about broken heterosexuality. Everything is broken in this world after the Fall. Everything about our sexuality—our attractions, desires, and behaviors—are impacted by the Fall. The sexual boundary laws in the Bible are for everyone. So when you use Scripture to help someone examine this subject, do you shine the light of God's Word into your own heart? Do you acknowledge that everyone, including yourself, needs to obey what it says, and that everyone, on some level, struggles in the area of their own sexuality? No one has been untouched by sin and struggle in this area. In all these discussions, you should always examine your own areas of sexual brokenness and confess ways you, too, have lived outside God's boundaries. Ongoing repentance produces the humility needed to enter into these discussions.

3. Acknowledge that the Bible is, in many places, not the easiest book to understand. It was written thousands of years ago; most of us read a translation from the original languages; there are sixty-six different books in two major sections that make up the Christian Scriptures; and there are places, events, and customs from those times that sometimes strike us as being quite

foreign. Nevertheless, the church throughout its history has submitted to the Bible as being the essential text that guides our faith and life. Scripture attests to itself as such: "All Scripture is breathed out by God and profitable for teaching, for reproof, for correction, and for training in righteousness, that the man of God may be complete, equipped for every good work" (2 Timothy 3:16–17).

No Christian can, with integrity, affirm any action or behavior without reference to Scripture. While the Bible is a series of texts embedded within a certain time and culture, Christians have always affirmed that it is a "trans-cultural" word, divinely inspired and able to speak to every generation regarding who God is and how his people are to live.

To examine whether or not something is permissible, an honest wrestling with Scripture has to be the starting point. Its message, its point of view, must be first and foremost. "For the word of God is living and active . . . discerning the thoughts and intentions of the heart. And no creature is hidden from his sight, but all are naked and exposed to the eyes of him to whom we must give account" (Hebrews 4:12–13).

Study the Bible, read books and commentaries, and don't be afraid to read scholars who take differing views on the subject. You learn more by trying to understand both sides. Isn't that how you love someone you are trying to understand—by listening and asking questions?

4. Love and respect those who don't agree with your viewpoint. We are called to both "rightly handle the word of truth" (2 Timothy 2:15) and "not be quarrelsome but kind to everyone, able to teach . . . correcting his opponents with gentleness" (2 Timothy 2:24–25). We should do this all the time. But on this topic it's even more necessary. We live in an ultra-sensitive age. People have seen the damage done by rhetoric that has fostered abuses by one group against another and have become much more vigilant (often hyper-vigilant) about how we communicate. In this atmosphere, disagreeing with what someone else believes, thinks, or does is frequently labeled as either hate speech or an act of shaming someone. It often feels as if no one is allowed to express opinions, say any behavior is wrong, or disagree with others.

What's happening here? As a culture, we have become a people desperate for acceptance. As Western culture has moved more toward the individual as the primary point of meaning and fulfillment, truth is now defined as one's own personal story. There are no longer any agreed-upon moral standards by which behavior can be measured, so we refuse to believe that there's anything wrong with us. There are opposite and different worldviews clashing on this subject. The Christian worldview is that man is in a desperate condition, needing rescue and restoration by Jesus Christ and his death and resurrection on our behalf. The secular worldview believes that we are all essentially good, in need of no help or rescue—only needing more personal freedom to fully authenticate the self. These two worldviews are incompatible at their core. Conflict is inevitable.

While worldviews are clashing, remember that there are also many personal issues at stake. When engaging with those who identify themselves as gay or lesbian, or wish to support people they know who identify as such, understand that the historic, orthodox view is one that makes a claim on them. Recognize that to turn away from an identity or life in which one has found personal meaning and support and love is no small matter. So sensitivities are high. Don't just engage the subject; get to know and love the person you are talking to. There may be no way to avoid conflicting emotions on this, but real love for another person can go a long way toward establishing mutual respect on both sides, even when disagreements remain.

Commonly Disputed Passages

Once you have laid the groundwork of love and respect for the other person (and hopefully agreed upon the primacy of the Scriptures), you can begin to have a more productive conversation about what the Bible actually has to say on the subject. There are six passages in Scripture that directly mention homosexuality (but several other passages that touch upon it indirectly). Three of these passages are found in the Old Testament (OT): Genesis 19:1–9 and Leviticus 18:22 and 20:13.

Genesis 19:1–9

When people with opposing viewpoints on homosexuality interpret Genesis 19:1–9, the story of Sodom and Gomorrah, there is often confusion and misapplication on both sides. In the story, two angels enter the city of Sodom to visit Lot and urge him to flee the city because of the impending judgment of God against it. God has declared the city to be wicked and irredeemable. As the visiting angels seek shelter in Lot's house for the night, the men of the city surround the house and demand that Lot turn over his visitors to them for their sexual pleasures.

> But before they lay down, the men of the city, the men of Sodom, both young and old, all the people to the last man, surrounded the house. And they called to Lot, "Where are the men who came to you tonight? Bring them out to us, that we may know them." Lot went out to the men at the entrance, shut the door after him, and said, "I beg you, my brothers, do not act so wickedly. Behold, I have two daughters who have not known any man. Let me bring them out to you, and do to them as you please. Only do nothing to these men, for they have come under the shelter of my roof." But they said, "Stand back!" And they said, "This fellow came to sojourn, and he has become the judge! Now we will deal worse with you than with them." Then they pressed hard against the man Lot, and drew near to break the door down. But the men reached out their hands and brought Lot into the house with them and shut the door. And

they struck with blindness the men who were at the entrance of the house, both small and great, so that they wore themselves out groping for the door. (Genesis 19:4–11)

This graphic and well-known story has sometimes been used by conservative Christians to broadly carica-ture the gay community as being out-of-control, lustful people who are principally consumed by a desire to have sex. Since that is what they see as the reason for Sodom's destruction, they view all gay people as also awaiting judgment and destruction. Viewing gays and lesbians through the lens of this one biblical story has resulted in Christians demeaning and even demonizing gays and lesbians, reducing them to almost less than human status.

The reality is far more nuanced. No one group of people has a corner on being lustful and sexually-obsessed. Heterosexuals are equally capable of being sexually pro-miscuous and out of control (think college students on spring break, as one example). Gays and lesbians are also interested in loving relationships, companionship, love, and family. That is what drove Jared to abandon his orthodox scriptural position and adopt an alternative interpretation. He wasn't just interested in sex; he wanted a relationship, someone to love and care for.

The pro-gay, alternative interpretation of Genesis 19 brings a different, one-dimensional slant to the biblical text. This alternative view sees the story as one of violence, of rape. In addition, proponents bring in Ezekiel 16:49, which states that the sin of the city of Sodom was its arrogance and prosperity, a prosperity based on economic injustice that ignored the poor and needy. Therefore, homosexuality was not the reason for Sodom's judgment and subsequent destruction, because it was not describing loving, committed, and consensual same-sex relationships that we know to be possible today. This view tends to see Christians who hold an orthodox perspective as predominantly singling homosexuals out for unfair treatment and discrimination.

So we see that both sides have their slant on the text. On one side, homosexuals are broadly painted with one large brush stroke as being "those kinds of people"; on the other, they are entirely painted out of the picture. Both sides bring an element of distortion to the argument. Those on the orthodox side must see gays and lesbians as being people just like anyone else—men and women made in the image of God who share deep, personal values the same as any other group of people. Pro-gay advocates, however, must not erase or ignore the data that is inherent in the story. While it is a story of violence and intended rape, the fact remains that homosexual sex was an elemental part of the intended violence, evidenced by the fact that Lot was even willing to offer his daughters in the place of the two men. That is highlighted by the references to Sodom in Jude 7 and 2 Peter 2:4–10. It's a pretty sordid story overall, and it probably isn't the best example for articulating the orthodox view of homosexuality, but it is a good example how each side sees elements in the story that support their limited viewpoints.

Leviticus 18:22 and 20:13

> You shall not lie with a male as with a woman; it is an abomination. (18:22)

> If a man lies with a male as with a woman, both
> of them have committed an abomination; they
> shall surely be put to death; their blood is upon
> them. (20:13)

A plain, on-the-surface reading would seem to raise this question: why is there any controversy over this matter? Homosexual relations are prohibited and condemned. On the other hand, the more we consider God's law, the more questions arise as to how to apply it today.

The pro-gay, revisionist side sees these two OT laws as either being outdated for today, or specifically limited to homosexual practices associated with pagan religious rites. As such, neither says anything about the kind of homosexual relationships we can observe today (committed same-sex marriages).

One way to dismiss these two laws is to relegate them to a bygone era. It is popular to hear people say that traditionalists pick and choose which OT laws they think are still relevant—like the prohibitions against homosexuality—while at the same time ignoring laws about wearing clothing with mixed fabric or stoning people who work on the Sabbath. Those who make this argument say the lack of consistency exposes what is really at work here: prejudice against gays and lesbians. In addition, some point to texts like Hebrews 8:13, which says that the old covenant was made obsolete by the coming of Christ. The OT laws were for Israel at that time; Jesus abolished the law, and his central ethic of love now liberates us to embrace those who were at one time marginalized and oppressed because of the culture.

There are a number of responses to these alternative arguments.

1. **OT Law is comprised of different parts, and understanding this is critical.** One of the most basic rules of biblical interpretation that has been held for two millennia (in understanding how the OT connects with the NT) is that Jesus's coming made the OT civil and ceremonial laws obsolete (that is, those laws that governed Israel's theocracy and their worship at the tabernacle/temple). Why just these two aspects of the law, and not the moral law? Because Jesus is now our "Temple," the place (now a person) where God and man reconcile and meet (see John 2:19–21). The elaborate worship rules in the OT regarding animal sacrifices for the remission of sin, and the rules regarding "clean" and "unclean," were fully met by Jesus's sacrifice on the cross. By Jesus fulfilling all the law on our behalf and sacrificing himself in our place, he made us "clean," that is, acceptable to a holy and just God. The OT sacrificial and ceremonial rules pointed ahead to Jesus. Now that Jesus has come, they no longer apply to us.

   So orthodox proponents do not arbitrarily "pick and choose" which OT laws to abide by. In understanding how the Bible is read through the lens of Christ's life, death, and resurrection, theologians have long understood that some laws were fulfilled and they simply no longer apply to us today. That is the reason the New

Testament (NT) is full of passages that explicitly mention the annulment of ceremonial laws and worship practices (regarding issues of worship, food, cleanliness, diet, high holy days, etc.). It was important for Christians to know that such laws were no longer relevant. But the NT noticeably lacks even one single mention or reference to the prohibition against homosexuality being removed. Why is that?

2. **The OT moral law continues into the NT because it reflects God's holiness.** It is because the moral laws, applicable to a people who belonged to God, still remain. So it is not surprising that the numerous passages in the New Testament that talk about sexual behavior among Christians, and the importance of conforming our sexuality to God's design, echo the OT's call to holiness.

For this reason, all the other sexuality laws in Leviticus are still applicable today. If Jesus's coming abolished the prohibition against same-sex relationships (because he abolished all the law), then for consistency's sake, he has also abolished the laws against incest that are in the same chapter in Leviticus. But if that were so, why did Paul get so upset at the man in the Corinthian church that was sexually involved with his father's wife (presumably his father had died)? And why was he so upset at the church, which adopted a position of tolerance toward such behavior? It was because he was applying Leviticus 18:8, which was still relevant for the emerging Christian church (for the story, see 1 Corinthians 5). The immediate context for Leviticus 18:22 and 20:13 includes not only laws against beard-trimming and mixed-weave fabrics, but also prohibitions against theft and deceit (Leviticus 19:11), against slander, hatred, and revenge (19:16–18). Yet no one argues that such morals are now obsolete because of the work of Christ. Rather, both the principles and the particulars are reiterated and reinforced under the New Covenant.

3. **Jesus strengthened the moral law of the OT.** Jesus, while fulfilling the law on our behalf (he lived perfectly the life we failed to live), actually strengthened the OT moral law, especially when it came to sexual behavior. We see this in the Sermon on the Mount, where Jesus reinforced and deepened the OT law against adultery by including lust of the heart (which is a secretive behavior) as equally a sexual violation against God's design. It's also seen in his tightening of divorce law in light of Genesis 1 and 2, where, in effect, he limited an almost limitless supply of sexual partners for those who abused easy divorce laws. Jesus did not reduce God's standards. The law was given to expose us to the real nature of our sinful hearts and drive us to God to find life in honest confession and repentance.

4. **Jesus aligned our sexuality with what the OT positively describes.** One of the most remarkable facts about Jesus is that throughout the

Gospels, he declared his love for and dependency upon the Scriptures. Over and over, in response to controversies and disagreements with the religious leaders, he declared, "It is written." In one encounter with the Pharisees (over the question of divorce), Jesus described the ideal of marriage by appealing to God's creation of humanity into male and female (see Matthew 19:3–6, where Jesus refers to Genesis 2:24). By appealing to God's creational order—before the Fall—Jesus is affirming God's boundaries for sexual expression as being only permissible between a husband and wife. Jesus agreed with this understanding of marriage and sexuality, which was not in doubt.

Those who want to override what both the OT and the NT say about God's design for our sexuality (by saying that the biblical writers didn't know about the kind of homosexual relationships we know of today), face a serious question when it comes to Jesus. Was Jesus so limited by his time and culture that even he was wrong on this matter? If so, then Jesus's understanding of the OT and how it applies to his followers is deficient, since he relied on its text without hesitation or qualification. Jesus's "silence" on homosexuality does not fit an interpretation that he would affirm mutual, loving, covenantal, same-sex relationships; rather, it says far more about his complete agreement with the OT Scriptures and its boundaries for sexual expression.

5. **Modern culture does not trump the culture of the Bible when it comes to what is wrong with us.** Those who argue for the acceptability of same-sex relationships say the biblical writers didn't understand the nature of homosexuality, while now we have knowledge in science and the social sciences that they didn't. While we can agree that the Bible is not a science book, and that even the book of Proverbs points us in the direction of using wisdom and experience gained from life in order to live rightly, we cannot ignore this one fact about the Scriptures: It is a book that is authoritative on the human condition. It tells us what is wrong with humankind, and how God is fixing the whole world through Jesus's life, death, and resurrection.

When any given time or culture subordinates what Scripture says about humankind and its condition in favor of current opinions, we run the risk of throwing out portions of Scripture we don't like. If we do this, we must then ask ourselves why we believe anything God has said about how we should live. The Scriptures warn us that our hearts all too easily fall prey to self-deception; they will delude us into affirming whatever we think is right for us.

6. **When interpreting these two passages it is good to take a wider view of the Bible regarding OT law.** Why were there so many laws for God's people to obey? The answer is because everyone—including the people of God—has

an innate, sinful inclination to live life apart from God in opposition to his ways. Without clear instruction everyone would do whatever they thought was "right in his own eyes" (Judges 17:6). The result, which the Bible thoroughly describes, is discord, more suffering, more death, and human misery. Sin is a destructive force that lives inside every human heart; it is a stance of the human heart that fundamentally disbelieves God and refuses to obey and trust him. To live rightly, we cannot look to our own hearts, for we are masters at self-deception. When it comes to knowing and living rightly with God's gift of sexuality, we need clear direction regarding its use because sexuality is primal and powerful and easily prone to destructive misuse. Boundaries are given for safety and to preserve what is good from what can corrupt. The law was a "tutor" that showed us how to live, but it was only when Jesus came that we would be given a new power to obey (the Holy Spirit).

The Broader Perspective of Scripture
Genesis 1—3

Another crucial way to understand the two Leviticus passages (and, in fact, all of the other passages in Scripture that speak directly on homosexuality) is to first read them through the biblical lens of the first three chapters of Genesis, where God made humanity in two genders and commanded them to unite sexually in marriage for the benefit of the whole world.

Genesis 1 and 2 acts as the foundational structure for all of creation, like a good foundation supports the whole house. What we read here is considered normative. Genesis 3, however, tells us how the foundation started to break and come apart because of the Fall of Adam and Eve. After Genesis 3, whatever "is" cannot be declared "normal" anymore. Following the Fall, man and creation have been in a continual state of disorder and disobedience.

When we read of the creation of Adam and Eve, we see that God created mankind in two genders. Sexuality is at the core of who we are. And men and women, though equal in being image-bearers of God, are different in so many ways. Male-female complementarity and gender differentiation is clearly displayed in these two chapters as the foundation for sexuality and sexual relationships. This is the way God intended his creation to function.

It is a profound concept to consider the differences between the sexes as the reason for sexuality. Theologically, the sexual union of man and woman is symbolic of the two split images of God (male and female) being reunited in sex. The differences between them, coming together in marriage, are intended to be a reflection of the intimate, joyful relationship among the Trinity that has existed in eternity. Unity and diversity, similarity and differences, come together. God uses what is earthy and physical to give us hints of what is divine and eternal about himself. In Ephesians 5:22-33, Paul describes marriage as a vivid illustration of God's relationship to the church. Here is another illustration that depends upon complementarity and differences; "same with same" loses the critical truth God wants to communicate to us about himself. Theology matters when it comes to sex and human relationships.

Physically and socially, the differences are crucial for one of the main objectives of sex: procreation. God never intended sex to be completely detached from procreation. And God intended sex to be confined within marriage—marriage creates a new family structure: "Therefore a man shall leave his father and his mother and hold fast to his wife, and they shall become one flesh" (Genesis 2:24). While sex was certainly created to be pleasurable (and God clearly approves of sex being so between a husband and wife—see Proverbs 5), the ultimate goal for sex was that it be combined with marriage for societal reasons, not purely personal or private ones.

Pro-gay advocates say the creation story in Genesis reflects only, at best, a predominant view of heterosexuality as normative. In other words, heterosexual sex is okay for most people, since most people are heterosexual, but for gay people, who have a different orientation, that's not possible. Therefore, since the passage in Genesis doesn't take that into account, same-sex relationships are permitted. A slightly different perspective on the Genesis story centers on what God said to Adam: "It is not good that the man should be alone; I will make him a helper fit for him" (Genesis 2:18). This argument is that God calls everyone to intimate companionship, and for gays, that's only possible with a person of the same sex.

Those two alternative interpretations seem clearly forced upon the text. The first two chapters of Genesis cannot be split off from Genesis 3, where sin enters the entire created order and what seems right and natural to man no longer equates with what God calls good and right. The argument that homosexuality is part of the created order, and that heterosexuality is merely the majority position that God created, simply cannot be found in this or any biblical text. And to interpret the "helper" passage as approving the acceptability of homosexual relationships, based on God's concern for the right companion for Adam, misses the plain reading of the text. This passage is describing humankind in general, and here God introduces Eve as the sexual opposite to Adam, and in doing so, establishes heterosexuality as the basis for the divine institution of marriage (that is what Genesis 2:22–25 is all about), and heterosexual marriage as the basis for bringing children into the world. The "helper" passage cannot mean that it should be applied to every single human being who lived, and that such companionship can be according to his or her sexual preference.

From the very beginning of the Bible all the way through to its end, the union between a man and a woman is presented as normative. You will not find a single passage that presents an alternative pairing of man-man or woman-woman as being permitted or seen as being positive.

Let's examine three New Testament passages that also directly mention homosexuality: Romans 1:18–32, 1 Corinthians 6: 9–11, and 1 Timothy 1:8–11.

Romans 1:18–32

> For the wrath of God is revealed from heaven against all ungodliness and unrighteousness of men, who by their unrighteousness suppress the truth. For what can be known about God is plain to them, because God has shown it to

them. For his invisible attributes, namely, his eternal power and divine nature, have been clearly perceived, ever since the creation of the world, in the things that have been made. So they are without excuse. For although they knew God, they did not honor him as God or give thanks to him, but they became futile in their thinking, and their foolish hearts were darkened. Claiming to be wise, they became fools, and exchanged the glory of the immortal God for images resembling mortal man and birds and animals and creeping things.

Therefore God gave them up in the lusts of their hearts to impurity, to the dishonoring of their bodies among themselves, because they exchanged the truth about God for a lie and worshiped and served the creature rather than the Creator, who is blessed forever! Amen.

For this reason God gave them up to dishonorable passions. For their women exchanged natural relations for those that are contrary to nature; and the men likewise gave up natural relations with women and were consumed with passion for one another, men committing shameless acts with men and receiving in themselves the due penalty for their error.

And since they did not see fit to acknowledge God, God gave them up to a debased mind to do what ought not to be done. They were filled with all manner of unrighteousness, evil, covetousness, malice. They are full of envy, murder, strife, deceit, maliciousness. They are gossips, slanderers, haters of God, insolent, haughty, boastful, inventors of evil, disobedient to parents, foolish, faithless, heartless, ruthless. Though they know God's righteous decree that those who practice such things deserve to die, they not only do them but give approval to those who practice them.

The revisionist interpretation of this passage has some of the same themes that were applied to the Leviticus passages and Genesis: that the culture of those times lacked what we know today, and that the interpretation centered on the meaning of a word or two. Here, the word *natural* and how that one word could be applied to the culture of that time is a major focus. Two times Paul says that "women exchanged natural relations," and "men likewise gave up natural relations," in favor of same-sex behavior. According to this argument, what Paul is upset about is men and women, who are really heterosexual and engage in homosexual sex, which would be "unnatural" for them. It would *not* be unnatural for gays and lesbians to engage in sex with the same gender.

This interpretation raises an obvious question: why would heterosexuals do that? Well, this interpretation says Paul is referring to men and women who are engaging in sexual behavior as part of a cultic act of worship; in other words, as part of temple worship of the pagan gods that society believed in. So what is being condemned is idolatry and unnatural sexual expression that goes against one's orientation. Some pro-gay advocates also say that Paul was here criticizing exploitative forms of homosexual behavior (pederasty, prostitution, idolatrous cults) or sexual behavior that is promiscuous or excessive (non-covenantal, non-monogamous), and that he knew nothing of the orientation understanding of sexuality that we now know.

The orthodox argument looks at the passage in its wider context. This view says that Romans 1 cannot be read as being merely a culturally dated diatribe against homosexuality. In fact, the point Paul is trying to make is not exclusively about homosexuality at all, but about humankind's fallen condition and how, throughout history, men and women distort the knowledge of God in order to live any way they wish. Paul is building an argument for why God had to become a man, Jesus Christ, in order to rescue us from our bondage to sin. This critical part of Romans is where Paul begins his argument to show that fallen humankind lives, not for God, but for a virtually limitless number of idols they have created (vv. 22–23), in an attempt to make life meaningful apart from the true God. This argument does not end with chapter one, but concludes two chapters later (Romans 3:21–26), where Paul shows that Jesus's death on the cross in our place was the only way we could be rescued and set free, by Christ's free grace to us, to live for God and begin again to experience life as God intended it to be. Jesus needed to break into history to begin a new world, the Kingdom of God, which is to this day breaking into the old world and restoring what is broken.

Paul uses homosexuality here as a vivid example to show how every human society and culture since the Fall is corrupted by sin and disorder. This is why he also lists more than twenty other sinful behaviors that are characteristic of humanity, in verses 29–31, to prove his point.

We were created to worship and live for God, but since sin entered the world and severed our original relationship with God, the human heart's default mode is still to worship something. The fallen human heart exchanges the worship of the true God with anything and everything else that people erroneously believe will make sense of life outside God's revealed will (v. 23). The result is human brokenness and societal discord (vv. 29–31).

This means that homosexuality is one of the characteristic behaviors of fallen man. It is not the worst of all sins (it is wrong, by the way, to use this passage to single out gays and lesbians for special condemnation) because Paul lists several other sinful behaviors that express idolatrous hearts. Because human sexuality is an aspect of creation that so directly mirrors the human relationship with our Creator (Genesis 1:27–28), it is not surprising that the effect of sin's entrance into the world would reach as deep as the level of human sexuality. Nothing has been untouched by the Fall, and even that which is so fundamental to being human eventually is used in ways that invert God's intended design.

It is important to mention here what Paul means when he says men and women were being given over to same-sex behavior (and again, the other behaviors of vv. 29–32). When Paul says, "God gave them up" in verses 24 and 25, he is referring to the freedom that we have to live in rebellion to his ways. When we give in to what our hearts desire—when we live for what we think we need in life (which is another way of saying that what we live for is what we worship)—then God allows these desires to control us. Like a child demanding his way, we get what we want. However, we get more than we want: To live one's life outside God's will and in opposition to it will both deepen our estrangement from him and will ultimately signal a tragic desire to live apart from him forever.

During the time of Paul, same-sex relationships, even long-term ones, were not uncommon. In the Greco-Roman world, which Paul extensively traveled, there were poetic tributes to male-male love and man-boy love, along with erotic love between women. Philosophers even discussed whether homosexuality was fixed or variable, debated its origin, and argued and discussed sexual orientation as people do today.[1] Paul was not an uneducated man; to say that he knew nothing of sexual orientation (although that word was not used) or monogamous same-sex relationships is to sell him short. Paul's view of human nature was extraordinarily deep. His view of sin and idolatry was comprehensive. Sin is not just a superficial deviation from an otherwise intact human condition (a mental "mistake" or error of judgment), but a complete breakdown of everything about us, including our physical bodies, down to the level of our biology.

Finally, as for the revisionist interpretation of the word *natural*, when Paul says twice that "women exchanged natural relations" (v. 26) and "men likewise gave up natural relations" (v. 27), he is referring to what is natural within God's created order, not what is customary for that particular culture. This is made clear in the words Paul uses in verse 23 to describe idolatry (which is exchanging the worship of God for something else). Paul's reference to "birds and animals and creeping things" is a direct allusion to Genesis 1 and the creation story. Paul is stressing here that what is natural (what was God's original, created intent for human sexuality) has been inverted and now proclaimed as being normative and acceptable (v. 32).

Again, the bottom line for Romans 1 is Paul's *gospel* argument, that "all have sinned [irreligious and religious, the sexually immoral and the religiously self-righteous] and fall short of the glory of God," and yet we can be brought near to God, be a forever-part of his family, by being "justified by his grace as a gift, through the redemption that is in Jesus Christ" (Romans 3:22–24). That offer of life is for everyone.

1 Corinthians 6: 9–11

> Or do you not know that the unrighteous will not inherit the kingdom of God? Do not be deceived: neither the sexually immoral, nor idolaters, nor adulterers, nor men who practice homosexuality, nor thieves, nor the greedy, nor drunkards, nor revilers, nor swindlers will inherit the kingdom of God. And such were some of you. But you were washed, you were sanctified, you were justified in the name of the Lord Jesus Christ and by the Spirit of our God.

1 Timothy 1:8–11

> Now we know that the law is good, if one uses it lawfully, understanding this, that the law is not laid down for the just but for the lawless and disobedient, for the ungodly and sinners, for the unholy and profane, for those who strike their fathers and mothers, for murderers, the sexually

immoral, men who practice homosexuality, enslavers, liars, perjurers, and whatever else is contrary to sound doctrine, in accordance with the gospel of the glory of the blessed God with which I have been entrusted.

Both these passages are similar and use some of the same language, so we can look at them together. On the surface, the meaning of the text seems clear. Like his argument in Romans, Paul gives a list of behaviors that, lived consistently and unrepentantly, show one as being outside God's kingdom. But also like the Romans passage, Paul proclaims the good news of the gospel to repentant sinners (1 Corinthians 6:11). The good news of the gospel is always preceded by the bad news of our lost condition; apart from Christ's grace, we live our way and not God's way.

The predominant revisionist interpretations of these two passages mainly revolve around the meaning of two Greek words, *arsenokoite* and *malakos*. *Arsenokoite*, which our English versions translate "men who practice homosexuality," is a word found nowhere but here. It is, in fact, a word Paul coined. Therefore, some conclude that we cannot be certain what Paul meant by this word, and at best he is most likely referring to homosexuality in the context of male prostitution. The other Greek word, *malakos*, which is translated as "effeminate" in some older versions is also found in Matthew 11:8. There it describes those in the royal courts who wear "soft" (i.e., "fine") clothing. Based on this connection with Matthew 11:8, some argue that the word is not clear enough to refer to same-sex behavior.

The revisionist arguments rely on the perceived ambiguity of these two words, and that we cannot know whether Paul was condemning all homosexual behavior or only that which was exploitative or religiously connected.

A closer look at the word Paul coined put two words together: *arsenes*, which means male, and *koite*, which means bed (the same word in Hebrews 13:4 that specifically refers to the marriage bed and thus has sexual connotations). In addition, many orthodox commentators argue that Paul appears to have used these two words together as a reference to Leviticus 18:22 and 20:13, where the Hebrew text also uses two words that translate as "bed" and "male." In combining these two words, and with its strong connection to the OT, Paul is reinforcing the comprehensive prohibition of homosexual expression that has been in place from the beginning.

But like his message in Romans, Paul offers deep hope to those who struggle with their sexuality. He speaks of those whose personal identities and loyalties have been transformed ("and such were some of you") and of how the salvation of Christ brings increasing wholeness and growth where there once was only rebellion and sin. What Paul says here touches on the issue of changed sexuality, which is a frequent misinterpretation of what Paul means here. For a good discussion of this, read David White's minibook, *Can You Change If You're Gay?* [2]

Conclusion

Many people conclude that the Bible is unclear or too dated to understand with any certainty whether homosexuality is permitted for God's people today. But if you truly look at these passages in light of the whole scope of sexuality as described throughout the Bible, and ground that view in the first two chapters of Genesis, then there really isn't any uncertainty at all.

The struggle over this issue is one that is far more emotional than rational. Wanting to be loving and on the side of inclusion, many will either dismiss what the Scriptures say or vigorously reinterpret them to come to another position.

Here is where one needs to step further back from the discussion on sexuality and look at the wider biblical message. Some interpret the entire message of the Bible as being centered in God's love for us, especially his love shown in Jesus. Whatever is loving among people, therefore, is something to celebrate, especially when it comes to including those who have been excluded or treated poorly throughout history.

This is only a partial truth. The central message of the Bible is about God's love, and that message is centered in what Jesus accomplished by his sacrificial death on our behalf. Love is defined by God. God's love is accepting, but it is a love that *intrudes* into our lives and transforms us. His love always disrupts us on the life-path we have personally chosen. His love is not the world's "unconditional love." His love is personal, intense, and relentlessly desirous that we become people who look and act like him. Look at 1 John 5:2: "By this we know that we love the children of God, when we love God and obey his commandments." If we are loving others the way we should, then we will also be obeying God out of a love for him.

The call to all of us is to live rightly and in harmony with God, loving our neighbor as ourselves. God is for us! That is why God came to earth and took on our humanity, so that we might know now, and in the life to come, the deep blessings that come from being in a personal relationship with him. For everyone, that will mean turning from those things in life we think we need and turning in faith toward him, listening and growing in obedience to his voice in all things.

Jesus said to Peter, when he wondered if following him was worth it in light of the personal cost to do so, that it truly was, for all eternity (see Mark 10:28–30). When Jesus says that we will receive 'a hundredfold' of "blessings in this life, his words are meant to exaggerate this fact: you will not be able to comprehend the richness and depth of [the life God will unfold to you] when you give yourself over completely to follow him and his Word."[3] Jesus knew what it was like to have people leave him because of his message, when our desires clash with God's ways. This is the ongoing conflict that faith always confronts, when the world and the flesh (see 1 John 2:15–17) can seem more reasonable than the ways of God. These words of Jesus remain strikingly relevant even today.

Endnotes

1. Dan O. Via and Robert A. J. Gagnon, *Homosexuality and the Bible: Two Views*, (Minneapolis: Fortress Press, 2003), 81.

2. David White, *Can You Change If You're Gay* (Greensboro, NC: New Growth Press, 2013).

3. Tim Geiger, *Your Child Says "I'm Gay,"* (Greensboro, NC: New Growth Press, 2013), 11–12.